PAULI MURPHY

Badass Consciousness

An Easy to Follow Guide to Becoming Totally Aware !

First edition

This book was professionally typeset on Reedsy.
Find out more at reedsy.com

Contents

Preface

Welcome to YOUR book !

This easy-to-follow guidebook will allow you, effortlessly, to become totally aware of, and to actually *know* who you are.

It will be a delicious and satisfying discovery of your formidable in-built Strengths and Skills.

This little book will uplift you - in Spades !

And *YOU* will have done it !

-About your Courage - Yes, YOUR courage !

I had the privilege of being a volunteer with a UK-based 'Helpline' for people who needed emotional support due to depression and stress, even up to the point of contemplating taking their own lives.

The major aspect of our training was to make sure that we don't EVER actually "give advice" (!)

In this way, we are able to help the Caller explore their own Feelings and so come to their own conclusions about what they needed to do next. (No-one ever wants to be told what to do !)

That will be my intention with this little book.

Well, what's that about Courage, then ? - Wait ! - Often, at the end of a Helpline Call I was told, "I cannot thank you enough for the advice you have given me." and I was able to respond,

"I didn't actually give you *any* advice. *You* had the Courage to pick up the phone in the first place and call a complete stranger. Then we both explored your Feelings and Emotions and *you* came to the conclusions about what to do next. - YOU did it, not me !"

So, Dear Reader, although you may not have thought much about it, it was YOU who decided to obtain this little book because you do indeed have the Courage to want to *explore* beyond the horizons of your current awareness and find out more about your **_innate_** Consciousness, which is indeed "Badass" as you will, to your delight and amazement, now discover !

I

Part One

1

How to Use this Little Book

-Your Boundaries.

It's high time that only *you* shall decide about what your boundaries will be.

All your life, you have been 'subjected' to boundaries that, for the most part, were established when you were very young, up to the age of about 7 or 8. During that time of our lives, we automatically trust and absorb what our parents, teachers, peers and friends tell us. If we have been fortunate, those people will have been, most oftentimes, well meaning and kind, and the boundaries that we subconsciously erected will have been mostly useful and benevolent.

Well, either way, it's now high time that **you** decided, - or continue to decide if you have already started, - just what your boundaries should be, according to **your** choices and decisions.

We won't explore those in any detail, yet, but here's one you can set right now:-

-Don't share this book (yet) with *anyone.*

You may have come across Esther Hicks, the widow of Jerry Hicks ? -

She has been, for many years, the channel for a group of Beings who gave themselves the collective name of Abraham[1]. More about them later. Jerry, who was a highly successful entrepreneur among very many other achievements, once gave this hugely helpful piece of advice, more or less in these words,

"Don't ever tell **anyone** about your plans until you have actually achieved them, or are very *seriously* on the way to, or very close to actually achieving them.

This is because even the most well-meaning friend or relative simply cannot resist trying to tell you what you should or shouldn't be doing, believing that what they are telling you is absolutely in your best interests."

Do make notes of what you would like to share, but keep them to yourself for now. However tempted you might be to enthuse about what you are discovering, even if you trust that person or persons to not *dream* of trying to 'tell you what you should be doing' - DON'T.

You'll be glad. That's a promise.

Here's who you CAN share your discoveries and enlightened moments with ->

Your **Higher Self** - who you will soon be meeting, if you haven't already

You see, your FEELINGS, your EMOTIONS, are your Inner Guidance System, even if you didn't realise it up to now...More on this later.

So, "gather up your skirts" and Roll On.

You might consider dipping, here and there, into the oncoming pages of this little book ?

Well, why the f*** not ? - It's your book !

Sure, why not bounce around the Chapters, seeing what appeals to you. However, you might consider making a note, somehow, of what you've looked into, so that you know where you have explored and what's not yet been revealed ?

Up to you, like *all* your decisions from now on. Right ?

2

What Is ?

lright, here we go ! - Hold on to your hat ! - PLEASE be open minded, as I know you know you are, - so you say !

Where did everything come from ?
It came from "All-That-Is"
What's *that* supposed to mean ?
Well, I'll just pop this idea in for you:-
You are immensely important.
You are an *essential* component, because, quite simply, without you, "All-That-Is" could not be All that it is. Right ?
OK, while you apparently exist, how do you know that you are alive ?
May I suggest that it could have something to do with the "Life Flow" of apparent "Energy" that truly seems to be flowing through you in your waking hours, gently "buzzing through your limbs and skin and nerves, allowing you to move, think, feel, see, hear, taste, touch, think-you-know and even fart and be aware !
So, where did it all come from ?
Never mind that for now, where did *you* come from ?

OK...

Imagine if *you* were "All-That-Is".

If you were that, then you wouldn't know what it might be like to *not* be "All-That-Is", would you?

So, in order to explore that possibility, you could decide to "split off" a part of your consciousness (Ah - there's that word !) to go off and try experiencing "separation", or "individuality" to see what that might be like ! - However, you would want to be sure that the part you split off could get back to you when it or you wanted it to, wouldn't you ? You would want it to be essentially inseparable, so that it could always be retrieved, would you not ?

You would also, I feel you can agree, be so entirely concerned and overwhelmingly filled with Love for that brave little aspect of you, - that aspect that you had decided to launch into the void of that brand new viewpoint of "All-That-Is" as a separate Being,- that you would love that little aspect so much that you would give It/Him/Her Freewill. There couldn't be **anything** more loving, could there, than to give someone *complete* Freewill ?

Consider this then:- Perhaps you are *indeed* an aspect of "All-That-Is" who is busy exploring an infinite panorama of infinite realms ?

More on this later.

3

Whence ?

There is, actually, *only* **Energy**.

There is nothing else. That's right, - nothing.

Even conservative scientists are now forced to agree that 'matter' doesn't actually exist, per se. We used to believe that Newtonian physics was part of the scientific 'bible', when we were told that electrons orbit the nucleus of an atom, but we now know that the electrons don't do that, but they actually pop into and out of existence billions of times per second instead !

So nothing truly exists for more than a tiny, probably immeasurable fraction of a second at a time.

The scientists now have to agree that everything in existence is, in fact, Energy, vibrating at myriad different frequencies, in order to *appear* to be solid matter or, indeed, any matter at all, physical or not !

So even *you* don't physically exist as you may have thought ! Every bit of your body is going in and out of existence all the time !

BUT - …..here it comes…..Your Consciousness is always present in your 'waking' state. (We'll talk about sleep and unconsciousness again)

If EVERYTHING is Energy, then where does Energy come from ?... before you consider the answer to that so obviously next question, let me talk to you to about the concept of 'channeling' after telling you a little bit about this Pauli Murphy bloke, who has written this book:-

Sent away to a Jesuit boarding school at the age of six and for the following ten years, Pauli is grateful to the 'blessed brothers' for having *beaten*, literally, every last vestige of religion out of him, giving him a wonderful start in life.

Not, perhaps, what the 'holy fathers' had in mind but it has served Pauli well, he feels.

He then ignored anything even vaguely 'spiritual' until he was introduced to Abraham[1] by his brother Christopher who lives in Santa Fé, in 2004.

Even then, Pauli presumed that it was all complete bulls*** until he found that there were other 'channels', such as Kryon[2] and Bashar[3] and others - more and more all the time - who were, and still are coming through with the *same information* and in many different languages, all around the world and all of it lovingly beneficial and for the highest good of all who are drawn to listen !

That got Pauli's attention.

There are, of course, charlatans in the sphere of channeling but you can always spot them, as they cannot resist a display of negativity of some sort. There are other, well-meaning channels, who unwittingly allow their opinions and preferences to 'colour' the information they bring, but you can detect an unstable frequency, a less than resolute vibration in their 'offerings'.

Your Discernment, guided by your Intuition, will guide you when you trust it !

To resume then, with the question, "If Energy is all that exists, then where does Energy come from ?" - The answer, given instantly by all the 'genuine' channels when asked the same question, which they often are, is:-

LOVE

Now just pause and think - Does that resonate with you ? - I believe you'll find that it does..?

If so, there you have it. SO simple as to be entirely beautiful as a concept...

EVERYTHING, - EVERYWHERE and EVERYWHEN comes from **LOVE**

"All-That-Is"/Source/God/Creator/The-Life-Energy-Flowing-Through-Everything/
Call-It-What-You-Wish all comes from, and returns to-> **LOVE**

4

Who Are We ?

R e. *You:-* Because you are a part of "All-That-Is", you are made from **LOVE** - you *ARE* **LOVE**
Whether you like it or not !
Re. *Others:-* This applies to ALL other sentient Beings also. Whether *they* like it or not !

"Everything", of course, includes the incredible Contrast that we can experience here on Planet Earth, the awful things which allow us to know what we *don't* like and which more easily allow us to know what we *do* like, and so we can *choose* - because of our fabulous gift of Freewill.

ALL of the 'genuine' channels are keen for us to realise that we are:-

Eternal Spiritual Beings, enjoying (or not...) **a chosen, temporary, Physical Experience, here on Planet Earth.**

Think about that for a moment or two...It's quite a revelation, is it not ?
Personally, I found it to be a massive relief when that truth finally

dawned on and resonated with me ! You always were, and you always will be, and you are eternally Loved.

So, (as Abraham[1] tells us) You can't get it wrong because you never get it done ! - You can always 'have another 'go'' Yay !

5

Who We Are Not

E go... - Get this:-> You are **NOT** your ego. The ego is a wonderful tool that we have been given, without which we would not be able to make judgements when they are needed. However, many make the terrible mistake of listening to their egos telling them total crap about themselves, which includes such as,

"Look, I have looked after you all your life so far and you are still *alive.* So I must know what I'm doing, Right ? -So believe me when I tell you stuff !"

Classic examples of this are 'The terrible need to be *right*' and another is of being led into the habit of instinctively looking at the 'negative' side of things. "Isn't Life Hell !"

The ego is, among other things, in charge of ensuring our physical protection from harm, and so it runs the "Fight, Flight or Freeze" aspects of our lives in physical form. Very necessary, especially when there are sabre-toothed tigers looking for you for dinner.

We will look into 'Sovereignty' later, but meanwhile bear in mind that your ego can very easily lead you into believing you are, or should be, under the **control of others** ('who know best, and/or who have *your* well-being foremost in mind...)

A nice example is the tale of a Harvard 'Professor' of English who was instructing his students about 'doubles'.

He explained that you can have a double negative, which resolves into a positive, such as,

"I can't *not* go to the funeral." but that, in the English language, you *cannot* have a double positive which resolves into a negative.

There was a long pause. Then a voice at the back quietly said,

"Yeah. Right !"

6

Universal Laws

Bashar[3] was asked quite recently in a channeling session if there are other Universes?

His answer was, "More than you have numbers to count!"

The next question posed was, "Are the laws of physics the same in these other Universes?"

And he replied, "No. But we are not going to 'go there' as they are too complex and you are not ready to explore such esoteric matters. However, there are Five Laws which pertain to all Universes, everywhere and everywhen. Would you like to know about those?"

Came the reply, "Does a bear s*** in the woods?"

Here is a précis of Bashar's 'revelation' :-

<u>The Five Laws of All Universes</u>

1. You Exist(Not much you can do about that, ever. You are eternal!)
2. The One is the All and the All are the One (We are, all, an integral part of "All-That-Is")
3. You get what you 'put out' and whatever you focus on expands

(Law of Attraction)
4. It is always Now (Time and 'place' are illusory)
5. Everything changes, except the previous Four Laws

7

Sovereignty

Your own sovereignty is inviolate, although you may not know it all the time, or even at all !
So is everyone else's, although the same things apply, - they may not know it...

Consider this:- You actually have no control, at all, over what anyone else does, says or thinks.

You may think you can influence them, or they you, and that is true but *only* if given permission.

OK, if someone is pointing a gun at you, you will quite likely give them that permission but the choice is always yours in any case, and also when those roles are reversed, of course.

From your non-physical perspective, before you came here, you understood that there is room enough in this expansive Universe, for all manner of thought and experience. You had every intention of being deliberate about your own creative control of your own life experiences, but you had no intention of trying to control the creations of others.

So, if you *don't* have that control over what anyone does, says or thinks, what *do* you have ?

The **only** thing that you do, actually, have complete control over in this, your physical life on Earth, is what you choose to think about, - you CAN choose your thoughts.

Therefore you have the ability to respond or to react (to what someone does, says or thinks) - or to do neither.

If you are choosing to respond, it makes a lot of sense to respond *only* from a loving (Kind) standpoint OR to choose not to respond *at all*, which can be an *equally* loving standpoint to adopt.

'Reacting' never works well. It simply ramps up a conflict. Fine, if that is your intention, but it doesn't usually serve you in any way.

8

Inner Guidance Systems

gain, even though you may not know it, you have, and everyone else has, an infallible Inner Guidance System called Feelings or Emotions.

It is this simple:- If what you are thinking about makes you feel **good,** then your Higher Self (your 'Inner Being', your direct connection to Source, or to call-It-what-you-wish) is thinking about that very same thing in the very same way.

Conversely, if what you are thinking about makes you feel **not-so-good,** then your Higher Self is **not** thinking about that very same thing in the same way.

As was said, the **only** thing that you do, actually, have complete control over is what you choose to think about. So, if you find that what you are thinking about is not making you feel good then you have the choice to change your thinking.

That's not always so easy, but the trick is to think of something else *-anything* else that you know it feels good to think about.

Imagine a situation when someone says something horrible and hurtful to you.

I have about five thoughts that I keep in my "back pocket", so-to-speak, and I whip one of them out when needed. They could be of a childhood friend, a wonderful holiday, a beautiful image, a fabulous taste, - anything will do, as long as you know it will make you feel better when thinking about it, and you only need to think of it for a very few seconds, because you can only think ONE thought at a time, even if only for a microsecond...

The unwanted thought *will* return - they always do - but here's the trick ! => they return, each time, with *less energy*; and return again, with *less energy*; and return again with *less energy;* until you wonder why you were ever bothered by it in the first place !

9

Heart Space

Your mind is *also* a wonderful tool, but, again, it is NOT who you are.

Your Heart, however, is the true center of your direct connection to your Higher Self, to Source. It is your physical 'portal' to non-physical, where the immeasurably greater part of you still, and always will, remain. It is from whence a part of you came into your present physical form, and to where that part of you, minus any negative aspects of your current personality, will return when your Soul chooses to transition from your present physical form back to non-physical at the end of your chosen life span. There ! - That's spelling it out for you, isn't it ?

Scientists have discovered and proved that the human heart contains approximately forty thousand neurons, so you do actually *think* from your heart, when you choose to !

The HeartMath Institute, (https://www.heartmath-dot-org)[4] established over 25 years ago have the following as their mission statement:-

"The mission of the HeartMath Institute is to help people bring their physical, mental and emotional systems into balanced alignment with their heart's intuitive guidance. This unfolds the path for becoming heart-empowered individuals who choose the way of Love, which they demonstrate through compassionate care for the well-being of themselves, others and Planet Earth"

Your "God-given" Intuition resides in your Heart Space. According to channeled information, human intuitive powers have increased a thousand-fold in only the last 100 years alone, so it is entirely reasonable now, to trust your Intuition completely. And it feels right and good to do so.

Those "gut feelings" we all have are to be respected and, unless severely influenced by subconsciously held limiting beliefs, are immensely valuable to us all.

(we'll look at 'limiting beliefs' later)

If you can 'imagine yourself' into your Heart Space at any time, it immediately feels different.

When I want to get into that Space, I imagine that I have an 'elevator' in my head.

Everyone can design their own elevator; girls tend towards rose-gold aluminum, mine has old-fashioned 'scissor-gate' doors.

When the need arises, I picture myself running across the inside of my head, into the 'elevator' and pressing the only button in there which is marked "H".

Slowly, I descend down through my neck onto my Heart Space, imagining my shoulders now to be above me, as the 'elevator' glides to a halt in the center of my chest.

Immediately, I feel more at peace.

I then take just a few slow, deep breaths, imagining they are coming in and out of my Heart, rather than my lungs, and even more peaceful feelings arrive and truly calm me down.

Whenever you want to think effectively, compassionately and/or lovingly, get into your Heart Space before you begin. Same for when you want to be creative and to "get in the 'Zone'"

10

Barriers

T he best bit of advice I was given by my best man at my first wedding was, "If you are blessed with children, then just make sure you stay friends with them - that's all that matters. They are going to do whatever they want to do anyway, so you might as well be pals !" Of course, he was absolutely correct.

I also remember saying to my son, when he was about four or five, "Who do you think is in charge of you ?" and he replied, hesitantly, "You are, Daddy ?"

I said, "No." So he said, "Mummy ?" and again I said "No." So he asked, "Then who ?"

And, to his obvious surprise, I told him, "*You* are. And you always will be !"

I like to think that that was when he realised that it was down to him to set his own barriers but of course we are born with that knowing, and it can be driven out of us by oftentimes well-meaning parents and teachers. This can be one of the subconscious, 'limiting beliefs' I referred to, and will again.

Your barriers are important, and *you* must set them, nobody else. They need to be set and reinforced from within your Heart Space, so that Kindness - to yourself and to others - is foremost in your considerations.

Others' barriers must be recognised and respected - though that can be effing hard !

11

Intention

Intention is probably the most important component of any and all activity, be it thinking, saying or doing.

If you can set your intention, (from your Heart Space, of course !) and keep it in mind, regardless of the 'bumps in the road' as you proceed, then it becomes the 'engine' behind your progress. Let go of your original intention and you lose your way and veer off track.

Easier said than done, but, with practice, it becomes easier and easier !

When setting an intention, it's really worth remembering that your Higher Self is always available to guide you, but - as with *all* 'celestial' Guides - they have to be **asked** ! - And they are *longing* to be asked, they can't wait ! - Well, they can, actually, they have infinite patience; - they need to have !

They will never interfere, and so will **only** offer guidance when asked. Asking out loud, if you feel able to, is a more effective way of communicating your request for assistance !

That guidance will come in different ways for each and every one of us. It could be an unexpected thought, a word or sentence on a roadside sign, an overheard phrase, an unusual feeling, *anything* ! - But you have to be alert to the answers you seek. Quieten your mind after asking and then pay attention. Again, it takes practice, but that's all it takes !

With respect to others' intentions, it's good to be clear about them. If you are not, then just *ask* them ! Most often they'll be glad you asked, as it means you are interested.

12

Communication

Understand that the person who transmits any communication is the person who is ultimately responsible for its receipt and its being understood.

If you created the 'message' that you want to communicate, then it is entirely up to you to ensure that it gets to where you want it to go, and is also understood, and, if necessary, acted upon ! If *your* message/instruction/ request/etc. fails to arrive or be heard or seen or be acted upon etc., then it's *your* fault.

Always. There are no excuses. Reasons, yes, but no excuse for a failed communication !

Keep that rule in mind and you can be sure that all your communications will be effective.

Don't hesitate to mention that rule to anyone with whom you wish to establish communications.

The best way to ensure that a communication has been properly received is to ask the recipient, politely, to repeat it back to you !

Receiving communications properly, and acknowledging their receipt is a kindness to the person or Being making the transmission and it also 'makes the World go around'!

Clarity is wonderfully satisfying, - and clean, clear communicating is a major component.

It is also a major contributor to Self-esteem.

13

Time

Time, in the non-physical, does not exist in anything like the way it apparently does in the physical.

Time has been given to us, mainly so that we have a "buffer" to prevent our making terrible decisions that could manifest instantly. If what we thought-we-might-want were to manifest in the very second that we thought of it, we could end up in the s*** very quickly !

That "buffer" of time, - the lag between when a thought is projected towards the engine of the Law of Attraction (see next Chapter) and when it actually manifests - gives us a chance to consider our projected thought and decide whether it was a good idea or not, and to change our minds before what-we-*thought*-we-wanted-but-don't-really-want arrives !

Remember the fourth Law of all universes ? - "It is always Now".

We are taught, correctly, that to be "present" serves us best; to focus on our "Now", which is all we actually ever have. Easier said than done, though.

So, when are we ever not in our "Now" ? ->Whenever we are engaged in thinking!

If you are successful at meditating, you are able to stop your thinking and find a place of real peace. You are truly in the "Now" and unbothered by ceaseless 'mind chatter'.

So, when you are engaged in thinking, your thoughts are *always* concerned with either the past or the future, have you noticed?

Of course it can be very useful to review past experiences and also to plan for the future, but the trick is not to get wedged in the mind chatter which can smother, embrace and kidnap your mind and reason...

We can learn from the past, but we cannot change it, it has *gone*, - so dwelling on it, if it doesn't feel good, is a truly stupid idea!

Planning, constructively, for the future is fine, but dithering about unarrived concerns and worrying about what might happen, is simply planning for things to go wrong!

Back we go to Feelings - is what you are giving your thought to making you feel *good*? - If not, think of something else, or even nothing, if you can.

Have you noticed that, when you are "in the Zone", doing something creative that you enjoy, time appears to cease to exist? Conversely, when time seems to be dragging, it's when you are definitely *not* enjoying yourself!

You have The Choice! - Yes, you bloody well do! - You are *not* under the control of others, unless you let them control you...(don't dwell on it, or it will become a habit and a part of your created reality - see the next Chapter) Read on!

14

The Law of Attraction (on a scale of 1 -10 of 'importance', this rates a full 10 !)

Many have heard of this so-called 'law', but not everyone truly understands it.

Pay attention, please, as it's *really* worth your while, while you are here.

Synchronicity brought you here, so trust the process !

Firstly, understand that we find ourselves in an Attraction-Based Universe - that means, there is no 'assertion', only attraction.

Nothing can enter into your experience unless you *let it* !

You create your own reality - ALL the time, mostly without realising it !

[If you've not heard about this before, don't 'sweat it', just follow along and you can contemplate it all later, and let it sink in without worrying. Remember, 'worrying is planning for things to go wrong' !]

Most people "create by default", unaware that they have the power, the immense power, to have their lives go the way they want.

They "react" to what they observe and place all blame insistently outside of themselves for whatever happens, miserably unaware of the fact that they are **not** 'victims'.

They have created their unwanted experiences by not realising that they actually have control, and by believing, completely, that they are, were, and always will be at the effect of what they observe. This very soon becomes a habit, especially if reinforced in early life by parents, teachers, peers and friends.

Even those striving for "awakening" can find themselves focusing on the **lack** of what they desire and so, inevitably, draw in further lack.

The Law of Attraction will always bring you what you give your attention to, whether you want it or **NOT** !!!

From the variety, and/or contrasts in this Universe, your preferences are born.

In the moment that your preference begins to exist, it begins to draw to itself - through the Law of Attraction - the essence of that which matches it. Then it begins an immediate expansion. This is how the Universe expands and this is why you have chosen to be on the leading edge of that expansion. The immensely valuable contrasts continue to provide the birthing of endless new desires and, as each new desire is born, Source Energy responds to that desire - it is a never-ending, always flowing, pure, positive energy expansion.

There are a few different ways of defining the Law of Attraction:-

"That which is like unto itself is drawn" is a rather old-fashioned description, but then the Law of Attraction has been around **forever** !

"What you put out, you get back" is another.

"What you focus upon gets bigger"

"What you give your attention to expands" and there are others, all describing that it is *up to you* what happens.

The very simple trick to getting it right is to ensure that whatever you are focusing upon for any length of time is something that makes you feel good, that it is something you desire and would welcome into your life. If it's not, then think of something else, **anything else** that feels better.

Again, don't 'sweat it' - If you worry about thinking unhelpful thoughts, then you are asking for more !

If there is something that you desire, then simply imagine, for a little while, what you will feel like when it gets here - and then **let it go** and think of other stuff - OTHERWISE, you will all too soon find yourself thinking about how and why it hasn't arrived yet, etc. and so keep it *away* ! Do you see ?

Again, don't 'sweat it' - just be glad that you are beginning to understand this essential Law and feel appreciation - *that* always works just fine !

15

Change

C hange is the *only* thing we can always be sure of. Our "job" is to make sure that the changes taking place within our lives are beneficial, to us and to all of those with whom we interact. So don't complain about change - it's going to happen anyway, so you may as well embrace it !

The scope of change is infinite and its arrival is consistent and inevitable, so "roll with it" and enjoy its Energy.

16

Synchronicity

You will have heard people say that there is no such thing as "coincidence", or that they don't believe in it, Yes ?

However, there are those who believe that coincidence and/or synchronicity are part of "The Divine Plan".

There are those, like me, who just don't know, but don't let it bother them either way.

I have found, however, that the "higher your vibration",(see next Chapter) the more frequently wonderful coincidences or synchronicities show up in your life.

17

Frequency and Vibration

Now that we know that *everything* is Energy it's worth recognising that all Energies exist at a given frequency or vibrational level.

You lower your own, personal vibrational frequency by being on the lower half of the emotional scale; you raise it by being on the upper half. Here is the Emotional Scale as explained by Abraham[1]

1. Joy/Knowledge/Empowerment
2. Passion
3. Enthusiasm/Eagerness/Happiness
4. Positive Expectation/Belief
5. Optimism
6. Hopefulness
7. Contentment
8. Boredom
9. Pessimism
10. Frustration/Irritation/Impatience
11. Overwhelment

12. Disappointment
13. Doubt
14. Worry
15. Blame
16. Discouragement
17. Anger
18. Revenge
19. Hatred/Rage
20. Jealously
21. Insecurity/Guilt/Unworthiness
22. Fear/Grief/Depression/Despair/Powerlessness

The easiest way to shift your vibration upwards is to be **Kind**.

Kind to yourself, first, and then it's easier to be kind to others.

This doesn't mean you have to be a "sanctimonious pillock" (to use a lovely phrase from the UK!) - it does mean that you have to think selfishly - yes, selfishly. What would be best for you.

What *would* be best for you is, quite simply, whatever will raise your vibration. Then, when you have been able to do that and, to some extent, maintain it, everyone you interact with feels the benefit, and you feel them feeling the benefit. Win-Win.

As you can only think one thought at a time, it is really worth choosing an uplifting thought (that makes you feel good) and then *milking* it, for all that it's worth.

That's all there is to raising your vibration. You can't maintain it all the time, of course, but if it is your *intention* to raise your vibration, then the Universe, - using the ever-active Law of Attraction, - will bring you whatever you need to achieve that, when you most need it.

Pipsy !

18

Beliefs

"A belief is just a thought that you keep on thinking" - (Abraham[1]) There are a variety of reasons as to why you hold a belief, i.e. keep on thinking whatever-it-is. The more you think about it, the more the Law of Attraction will bring you thoughts that match and reinforce it, until it is so obvious and apparent to you that you are telling yourself, "There ! - I told you it was true !"

It could be that it was impressed upon you as a child; it could be that it seemed logical and obvious to you; it could be that you can't actually say why you believe it - that is more common than you might think !

Your Ego will be busy doing its best to ensure that you continue to hold on to your beliefs, since it helped to form them in the first place. And Ego "cannot be wrong", it will tell you, and you are still alive, so it must be right, yes ?

Well, remember that your ego is not who you are, but it is a useful tool, when properly employed.

Beliefs, therefore, can be changed.

I'll give you an example (Flat Earthers please ignore this !)

Until various early Greek philosophers and their subsequent astronomers were able, not just to postulate, but also to prove that the earth is round (or rather elliptical) everyone believed that it was flat. Only when people were able to understand the proof that it is actually round, were their beliefs radically changed.

You may have been of the belief - or at least of the 'not knowing' - that there is no life before birth or after death and (possibly) even just reading this little book has provoked you into firstly questioning your existing beliefs and then to considering that the may be some truth to what has been put forward about Souls, non-physicality, Source and so on...?

Now those are conscious beliefs. We are aware of them.

We also have subconscious beliefs, which are far more "tricky" and can be what are known as "limiting beliefs".

Our subconscious is an absolutely enormous repository of knowledge, memories and wisdom.

Learning to unlock your subconscious mind will unleash your true potential and radically transform your life.

However, it is such a massive subject that I'm simply going to suggest that you do your *own* research on it and I believe that you will find it tremendously rewarding.

19

Judgement

Knowing that your ego is a tool, and not who you are, and that without it we would be unable to make judgements, means that you can utilise your powers of judgement with care and discernment and to great and beneficial effect.

When you observe something without judgement (difficult if you are habitually judgemental) you can obtain a clear, unbiased view and come to valuable conclusions, very quickly.

You will find your own way to avoid judgement without being told (we don't like to be told what to do, have you noticed !?) you will 'catch' yourself being judgemental and know what to do about it and it will be the best way for you - and it's nobody else's bloody business, anyway !

Letting go of judgement about *other* people who are being judgemental is probably the hardest - but it's possible, and actually very satisfying !

20

Stress and Anxiety

All illnesses are caused and exacerbated by an imbalance, such as stress or anxiety.

Your approximately 52 trillion bodily cells, each one of which have their own type of consciousness and which connect, consciously with each other (how do you imagine they cooperate to keep you alive ?) are constantly aware of how you are doing and reflect any upset that you are feeling by getting their 'panties in a twist' and going out of balance. Their collective intention is to draw *your* attention to the problem, and, if you fail to notice, they will ramp up the symptoms in order to try and attract your notice !

What's to be done about stress and anxiety ? - Be **KIND**. - to yourself, by doing whatever your Intuition and your guidance system (your Feelings) and your Guides, if you ask them, tell you to do.

That's it.

You *will* figure it out.

If you want to help someone else who has stress or anxiety, then you could do worse than quote the above to them, which would actually be very kind, and, if they choose to take any notice and do anything about it, both you and they will have succeeded in surmounting and meeting a massive challenge that you both chose to face.

21

Abundance

F irstly, be quite sure, money is not abundance. It often helps, but it can also screw up your life.

You know abundance from what your Feelings and Emotions tell you.

Once again, using the Law of Attraction brings abundance, but remember, focusing on a **lack** of abundance will bring you a guaranteed continuation of that very **lack** !

From the lower half of the Emotional Scale (ref. Chapter 17) such as being jealous of, or having a disapproving judgement of someone else's abundance, will also make sure it never reaches you !

What brings abundance, then ?

Visualising it. Using your 'God-given' imagination (the most powerful creative tool that you have !) to 'see' - and more importantly, FEEL what it will feel like when it arrives.

That's it !

THEN - let it go and think of something else, *anything else.* - Why ? Because the chances are extremely high that by continuing to think about it, you will slip into thinking about its not having arrived yet, and therefore keep it permanently *away* !!!

22

Courage and Audacity

YOU had the incredible Courage to decide to volunteer for a physical incarnation in this leading-edge environment called Planet Earth.

Furthermore, if you ever have any concerns about 'worthiness' or 'self-esteem', know that there were millions of Souls lined up to experience your 'job', what you have come here for, but that you were chosen out of all those millions - not by 'competition', but by the agreement among all those Souls that YOU were the best choice for this particular incarnation at this particular time !

Among your many other choices of personality and character for this time around on Planet Earth, you had sufficient Courage and Audacity to carry it off which is why you're here, now !

Don't doubt it ! - It's right there inside you, for when you need it, and you will never be offered a challenge that you are not capable of meeting.

"Oh, yes ?" you might say, "What about suicides ?" - Well, you don't even know your own 'Path' in this life, let alone anyone else's, so when anyone chooses to take their own life it will have been that Soul's choice

- and none of your business ! - and, back in non-physical, remember, there is no judgement, only Unconditional Love.

23

Gratitude and Appreciation

You know that the Law of Attraction brings you more of whatever you give your attention to ?

Well, then it is easy to realise that feeling and showing gratitude and appreciation will bring you more and more to be grateful for and appreciative of !

It's THAT simple, like so much in existence.

And it's SO powerful ! - Next time you meet someone with whom you really 'click', try deliberately feeling appreciation, consciously, and gratitude for the circumstances that brought that meeting about and imagine the future to be bringing you more of the same sort of friends.

I.E. Don't fall into the trap of "I wish I could meet and be friends with more people like this, but as I haven't yet, I'm not likely to do so..." That will keep them well away, won't it ?

My brother, Christopher, who lives in Santa Fé, coined the word, 'appreciatude' (pronounced a-preesh-a-tude) which combines the two. It can also dilute the possibility of one being a better idea than the other. It has been suggested that 'gratitude' contains a vestige of "thank heaven that's arrived and made the previous unwanted situation change or disappear" which reflects an aspect of 'lack', whereas 'appreciation' can be more pure, focusing on that-which-is-appreciated without reference to anything that it may have 'replaced'...Mmmmmmm...

24

Sleep and Unconsciousness

Apparently, according to the genuine channels, - and it resonates with me - when you are in deep REM sleep, you have actually, temporarily, left your body for it to rest on 'automatic' and 'recharge' while you return to non-physical and meet up with whoever you wish to, and to discuss everything and review your agreements and contracts and to do whatever you choose.

This keeps you well connected with non-physical, which is your earnest desire, be quite sure, on a daily basis. This could explain why sleep deprivation is so massively debilitating and soon leads to physical death.

This process also 'resets' your 'point of attraction' so that when you awake in the morning, if you choose to remember any dismaying thoughts that you may have been having the night before, then your vibrational 'point of attraction' will be right, slap-bang back where your dismay left off.

However, if you can begin your waking day with thoughts of appreciation - just a list of five little things will do, no matter how simple they might be, such as the warmth of your duvet or the very fact that you're still breathing ! - this will set your day off to a brilliant, brand new start with your vibration up, good and high.

Meditation is probably the best possible way to start your day, so even if it's just ten minutes of peaceful, thought-free relaxation, it, too, will shoot your vibrational levels way up.

Unconsciousness is, usually, the body's way of protecting you from experiencing unwanted and unhelpful trauma. It can often include forgetfulness of a situation, such as being run over by a bus (!) the terror of which would not be helpful for you to recall.

You will remember the bit that matters for safeguarding your future, such as seeing the bus approach. The whole Body and Soul complex is fantastically beneficial, and is worth feeling grateful for !

25

Self Love

Many feel uncomfortable when they come across that phrase. It seems self-indulgent ? Then try 'Love of Self' instead ? Knowing, as you do (don't you ?) that you are an integral part (or 'spark') of "All-That-Is" then it would be surly, surely, and even severely ungrateful to **not** have appreciation for who you are, wouldn't it ? This utterly fabulous gift of Life ? Feel that 'buzzing' in your body and know that it is the Life-Force-Energy flowing continuously through you !

Go, now, into your Heart Space and take a few slow, deep breaths, imagining those breaths coming into and out of your Heart, rather than your lungs.

So, - you can try turning any disapproval of yourself into an appraisal instead - an observation rather than a criticism - and, with that, a consideration as to how you could simply and positively improve things for yourself - and for others, while you're at it.

There is, according to many genuine channels, only really ONE RULE - Be **_KIND_**

Kind to yourself *first* - and then it's easier to be kind to others.

So, Love of Self is really the most important aspect to address. It's the seminal 'starting place'.

Then you can get right on and begin, fully, to live by :-

"The Basis of Life is Freedom; the Purpose of Life is Joy !"

And, the better it gets the better it gets !

26

Forgiveness

Back to "Self" - Forgiveness of Self must come first, then it is easier to forgive others.

Firstly, let's think about pre-birth agreements.

I now believe that we all take great care to plan our incarnations before we come, in order to make the very best of the opportunity. We get together with our wise Guides and our Guardian Angels and then our Soul decides which challenges and opportunities and experiences it wishes to engage with this time, in order to contribute most effectively to our expansion, and thus to the expansion of "All-That-Is".

Bear in mind that we **_always_** have Freewill and can decide differently to our pre-birth plans at any time, and change agreements, especially when meeting up with everyone during deep REM sleep each night. We might concur to 'tick that box' about a particular agreement and consider it dealt with, and let it go.

So, we make and reconfirm our agreements with other Souls sharing our journey.

Apparently, we all have a 'Soul Family' of 144 with whom we often reincarnate and switch 'roles', which is why you can often feel someone is very familiar, even a stranger in an occasional encounter.

We agree, when in the non-physical environments, as to what we can contribute to each other's life experiences and choose, or not, to put those agreements into effect as we go along.

Consider, then, the case of someone with whom you made an agreement so that you could experience being the butt of seriously hurtful verbal abuse or ridicule, and so that they could experience being a really horrible and mean accuser and critic.

When a person is being really horrible and mean, it is really not that difficult to bring to mind that *they* have the far more arduous 'job' of being nasty to you, by agreement, and so it becomes so much easier to forgive them, - and yourself for any reactions, - knowing that.

You will also find, as I have, that when you acknowledge such a situation within yourself, and forgive yourself and the other person, then most oftentimes that box will then have been 'ticked' and the same situation won't reoccur. You will both have fulfilled your contracts to your mutual benefit, and to "All-That-Is" in the expansion !

Sound too easy ? - Try it !

27

Conclusions

Where do you feel you are up to ?
Because, bear in mind, YOU did this !
YOU chose to read this little book.

You actually arranged for it to be written for you, although you didn't know that at the time.

We all chose to have a 'veil' drawn over our memories of previous lives (which, actually, are all happening simultaneously in the "Now", which is all we ever really have, but we won't go into that just now !) and the purpose of that 'veil' is so that we have the chance of making the very best of the opportunities we had decided to experience.

It's like young children watching a movie. They are 'right in there' with the characters and the actors, experiencing it as if it was entirely real, and for the most part, if it's a good movie, enjoying it far more than the adults who know that it *is* a movie, with actors, and not 'real' at all !

So, I hope you have enjoyed, and are intending to continue enjoying your 'movie' ?

I'm enjoying it enormously and I thank you, from the bottom of my heart, for agreeing to have me write this book.

I'm going to create a page on my website (https://www.paulimurphy.com) with FAQs and I would welcome it hugely, if you could post your questions and any comments you care to make.

   If you would care to 'subscribe' on my website, so that I may have your email address, I will promise to keep you posted, of course, and be very glad to have you 'on my list'.

Furthermore, and lastly for now, I will be **_enormously_** grateful if you would take the time to write a **_review_** of this little book on Amazon, where you found it.

Thank you !

You are more wonderful than there are words to convey, and I trust that you, too, now realise this - "In Spades" !

With Love,

Pauli

28

Acknowledgements (inc. Footnote Refs.)

Firstly:- YOU, Dear Reader
Secondly :-The Mikkelsen Twins (publishinglife.com)

Citations:-
a) The "Genuine" Channels
1Abraham (abraham-hicks.com)
2Kryon (kryon.com)
3Bashar (bashar.com)
b) Another Citation (not a Channel)
4The HeartMath Institute (heartmath.org)

Printed in Great Britain
by Amazon